Contents

Introduction

Can you imagine a world without instant messaging, texts and the chance to instantly post a picture of yourself online? Or a time when you couldn't find out where your friends had been at the touch of a screen? Well, that wasn't actually that long ago. Technology has moved at such lightning speed that sometimes it's easy to forget that once upon a time we didn't live our lives online.

Just take a look at these statistics:

* *4 out of 5 UK teens who own a phone, have a smartphone*
  *Ofcom
* *90% of phone owning teens send and receive texts daily*
  *PEW Internet and American Life Survey
* *The average teenager sends more than 3,000 texts per month*
  *Nielsen
* *80% of phone-owning teens take pictures and 64% share these with others*
  *PEW Internet and American Life Survey
* *73% of teens use social networking sites*
  **The Guardian*
* *An average UK household now owns three or more Internet-enabled devices (laptop, mobile, games console)*
  **The Guardian*

* *Teenagers especially are ditching more traditional activities in favour of their smartphone, with 23% claiming to watch less TV and 15% admitting they read fewer books*
*Ofcom

All this technology has transformed our lives for the better (despite the news headlines). We can stay in touch more easily, talk to our friends instantaneously (and cheaply) and basically have fun with people we know (and don't know) even when we're home alone. But with the ever-changing line-up of new gadgets, apps, websites and smartphones come problems and challenges, especially when you're a teenager. Problems such as befriending everyone who asks you, saying too much to too many people, being too accessible and posting pictures and words you can instantly regret. There's also the feeling that living somehow does not count if you're not documenting it online (not just a teen problem) and so the problem is getting the balance right between the digital and the real world.

If all of the above rings true and you're looking for some tips to ensure you don't give away too much, or help on how to deal with anything from mean behaviour online to not being able to wean yourself off your phone, then this is the book for you. ***Texts, Tweets, Trolls and Teens*** is all about helping you make technology work for you in the right way. **Give it a try – you won't be sorry.**

CHAPTER ONE

How are you using tech?

"I spend hours online. Do my parents know? I don't think so because I'm often on my phone while doing homework and playing games in my room. Even when I eat dinner I am texting."

NAT, 13

"I have a smartphone and laptop and I use my mum's iPad. What do I do online? What don't I do? – I do everything online, it's part of my life."

SARAH, 13

Are you super tech-savvy? If you are, you're not alone. Teenagers are amongst the most tech-savvy people in the world, knowing how to use technology to its best (and worst) advantage. So it's no surprise that around 85% of teens now have a mobile phone with the majority owning a smartphone, which allows direct access to the Internet. Alongside this around 90% of phone-owning teens send and receive texts daily, with one in three sending 100 texts or more. And the cherry on the cake is the fact that a huge

75% of teens use social networking sites daily in order to chat, flirt, relieve boredom and impress others.

With all this digital communication comes the fear from many adults and parents that teens are losing face-to-face contact and forgetting how to empathize. The good news is (as you already know) this isn't happening. Tech is just part of normal life for teenagers and far from making you less sociable, it's increasing networks of friends and increasing the amount you 'talk' and socialize. If anything it's just another way to talk to friends and share your life.

However, the online world comes with a whole load of pitfalls and disasters in the making. Dramas that get blown out of proportion, cyberbullying, text bullying, nasty pictures, horrible videos and people doing all kinds of weird things that you may not even have thought about before.

This is why it's so important to understand the sites and devices you're using and more importantly to check your tech behaviour. Whether that's thinking about who you're connected to and why, or considering how much time you really spend online and what you're actually doing when you're posting.

Keeping your tech behaviour in check is key to staying safe online. So here's what you need to know.

QuiZ What's your tech style?

1 *You have a great bit of gossip! What do you do with it?*

a Message all your friends instantly
b Post it on Facebook
c Post something full of hints but don't actually give it away

2 *Someone you don't know asks to connect on Instagram. What do you say?*

a Yes – but Google him/her first
b Yes – you're all about numbers
c It depends if he/she's connected to anyone you know

3 *Do you trust your online friends as much as your offline friends?*

a Some of them
b All of them – they definitely know you better
c Offline over online always

4 *When you feel upset your first response is always to...*

a Message all your friends
b Post your feelings on a social network
c Text a mate

5 *The majority of what happens online is...*

a Funny and silly
b Drama and gossip
c Interesting and private

6 *Mobile phones and social networking sites make...*

- **a** Life so much easier with friends
- **b** Life so much more complicated with friends
- **c** Life so much more interesting with friends

7 *The worst thing about tech is...*

- **a** When you run out of credit
- **b** When someone takes something you said the wrong way
- **c** When there's no Wi-Fi

8 *When your friends fall out online you're most likely to...*

- **a** Sit on the sidelines and say nothing
- **b** Be in the heart of it
- **c** Your friends don't do that

Mostly As You love your online life, using it to stay in touch with friends and have a laugh. You're aware of the pitfalls but when bad things happen you tend to ignore it and hope it will go away. You need to be more proactive in protecting yourself online and on your phone. Think about what you're doing when messaging and texting. Don't be part of the drama, as it could well backfire on you.

Mostly Bs For you, your online life and your offline life are one and the same! This isn't unusual but be careful not to become too caught up in things that happen online.

The online world is full of drama and angst as people tend to post their feelings openly. This means it's easy to be mean or say something you later regret. Keep the balance between the two worlds and remember if you wouldn't say it face-to-face, don't say it online.

Mostly Cs You have a great balanced tech style that means you have your feet firmly placed in the real world. You love the digital world but you're careful not to get too involved in all the stuff that goes on there. Instead, you stick to having a laugh, posting funny things and generally seeing what interests you before you post a reply. If someone gets too silly you back away or take it into the real world to sort it out. Good for you.

Who are you really connecting with?

"I fell for this guy online. We met through Facebook and started messaging like crazy. He really got me and I really got him even though he lived in California and I live in the UK. It was crazy for a while as we'd message all day and night, then he started to get jealous and asked me to delete all the boys on my FB profile and when I wouldn't he started saying all kinds of mean things about me. My mum made me block him instantly but he still tried to contact me through friends, then he found me on Instagram and he started name-calling again. It was horrible. I had to come off all the social networks for a while."

LARA, 14

"Yes I've had weirdo chats on gaming sites. People who say they're 14 and you can tell they're really adults. I just block them right away."

MAX, 13

To some degree we're all a little fake online. We want people to see us in a certain way and social media allows us to tweak our posts, be funnier than we are in real life and maybe embellish certain factors about ourselves. On the whole, the majority of people are who they say they are, but that still leaves a minority who aren't. And it's this minority that you need to worry about and be doubly cautious about.

Being cautious means being careful about who you friend, allow to follow you and who you chat to online. It's best to always check out the people first before you put them on your list. You may think it doesn't matter but it does. Anyone who follows you or friends you will have access to everything you share online, from private pictures and videos to personal information. Think of it this way – if you wouldn't let them into your house, don't let them into your social media accounts.

The reason for this (aside from not knowing their intentions) is that the online world makes us share more than we usually would. We can build relationships with people very quickly and feel closer to them than we actually are. If you allow others to friend you when you don't know who they are – because they look great or you're flattered they've asked – you're basically doing the equivalent of sitting down with a stranger and telling him your life story. On the whole this isn't a problem, but it can quickly become a problem if you fall out with someone you hardly know, or the people you are connected to have weird intentions (there are more strange people online than you might think).

Strangers aside, you also need to be aware that even your own friends can become problematic online. Some can harass you non-stop and not realize what they're doing, or start doing silly things like sending graphic videos that aren't funny to everyone on your timeline. Others can say strange things and then get upset when you reply, or don't. And others will quite happily air their dirty washing online in full view of everyone else. While you can't predict or change how someone else behaves online, you can control your own online behaviour. This means having your rules and boundaries that you stick to no matter what.

Some golden rules...

Rule One *If you have a problem with a friend, don't fight in full view online and draw others into it.*

Rule Two *If you see friends being mean to someone don't join in for a laugh.*

Rule Three *Don't post embarrassing pictures of other people you know. It will only open the door to this happening to you.*

Rule Four *Look at your privacy settings and ensure they are set correctly to protect your information.*

Rule Five *Think before you post anything. Even something seemingly harmless can offend others.*

Rule Six *If someone starts being silly or rude on your timeline ask them to stop. If they won't, block them!*

Rule Seven *If you're having problems in the online world, always tell your parents. Things can escalate quickly online, leaving you feeling upset and harassed.*

Rule Eight *If someone says something uncomfortable in a chat room, multi-player game or by text, immediately stop speaking to them and tell someone.*

Rule Nine *Don't spill someone else's secrets online – act as you would face-to-face.*

Rule Ten *Never share your passwords.*

Your behaviour online – avoiding the temptation to be mean

> *"Yes I've posted mean comments but it's just a laugh. People know that."*
>
> **TOM, 14**

Being online changes all of us. It makes some of us funnier, some of us smarter and some of us just mean. You can see this on blog posts – often there is just one person determined to be personal, unkind and nasty just for the sake of it. On social media it's also rife, especially when people post pictures or personal thoughts. This seems to open the door to people who want upset that person by being nasty, spiteful or making them feel small.

Sometimes this meanness becomes so consistent that the person doing it is known as a troll (see Chapter 5 for more on this). Famous people probably get the most spite and meanness thrown at them. People like athletes, singers, actors and actresses – anyone who dares to step into the public eye. However, trolls can behave like this to absolutely anyone.

Being mean is connected to the physical distance we have from the people to whom comments are directed. Studies show that the closer we are to people when we speak, the less likely we are to be mean-spirited.

If you read anyone's timeline you can see that lots of non-trolls, perhaps even friends, quite happily comment negatively on posts or pictures. Experts say this also has a lot to do with people forgetting that they are talking aloud to a lot of people when they post online.

Being mean can include of a lot of things. Here are some that you might have come across:

* *Being spiteful and sarcastic about someone's comment or picture.*
* *Sharing someone's picture with a 'funny' comment.*
* *Tagging everyone on a horrible picture of a friend.*
* *Being OTT with your view on a harmless comment.*
* *Being overly angry with someone online in front of everyone.*
* *Writing posts about friends where you don't mention them but it's clear who you are speaking about.*
* *Slating other people's likes and dislikes in an OTT way.*
* *Being overly critical of someone else's post for no reason except that it annoys you.*
* *Group texting a mean comment or thought about someone.*
* *Tweeting or posting about someone you're not connected to but everyone knows.*

The way to avoid being mean online is to always stop and think before you post. Consider whether you would make the same comment if your friend was standing next to you. If someone makes you angry or upset, stop and think whether a private message would be better than a public one. Think, would a face-to-face chat be better than a Facebook post? If you're having a text war with someone, would a bit of space and then talking in person be better?

The online world, while great for communication, is also a hotbed of misunderstandings and misinterpretations. It's a fast place where lots of people just don't think before they post and so disagreements and fights are easily ignited.

Don't be a part of the drama – stand back, think before you post and always resist the temptation to let your inner meanness out.

Gaming – what are you playing?

GAMING FACT *97% of 12 –17 year olds play computer, console, portable or phone games, and half of teens play on any given day, usually for about an hour. 94% of teen girls play games, as do 99% of teen boys.*

Gaming has come a long way in a very short space of time. Aside from being a multi-million pound business, today's game graphics are so sophisticated that they look better than some movies. What's more, the new games consoles and apps connect to the Internet and allow you to play with fellow gamers from all around the world. As exciting as this is, it also brings huge risks. The main one being that **you never really know who you are playing with.**

While this in itself is no bad thing, it's worth considering whether who you're talking to is real or not. The gaming world attracts a lot of people who become wrapped up in the games they are playing. The games can become violent very quickly, which means players themselves quickly become aggressive and angry. The best way to protect yourself is to pay attention to game ratings. If you say you're 18 when you're actually 13, you will be exposed to gaming elements and players that you obviously shouldn't be.

Protect yourself on multi-player games:

* *If another player is making you feel uncomfortable, back off and either stop playing or tell your parents what is happening.*

* *Learn how to block and/or report another player if they are making you feel strange or asking you uncomfortable questions. Keep a record of what the other player said, but do not engage them.*

* *Don't use a webcam while you play. Strangers don't need to know what you look like, and avoid voice chat to protect your anonymity.*

* *Protect your personal information. This includes your name, address, phone number, usernames and passwords, etc. One way to do this is to make sure the automatic share to social media options are switched off.*

Also, consider what you are playing. Many teens think it's fine to play games designed for adults that show you and encourage you to tackle things that you would never witness in real life, i.e. extremely violent and sexual content.

Yes, it's a game, not real life, but studies show that watching violent and sexual content has huge negative effects on everyone. Plus some adult games are designed to make you spend hours and hours on them and are highly addictive. For this reason, always be sensible about the games you choose to play.

In terms of ratings, PEGI labels appear on the front and back of computer games, indicating 3, 7, 12, 16 and 18 – these tell you whether or not a game's content is suitable and appropriate for your age. For example, PEGI 7 contains some possibly frightening scenes or sounds. PEGI 16 is applied once the depiction of violence or sexual content looks the same as it would in real life. Bad language, drugs and alcohol can all be included in games that are given a 16 rating.

How long are you online?

"My parents don't understand, I have to be on my phone all the time. I have to know what's going on."

ZOE, 13

While everyone feels they can't live without their phone, or games, or apps, you can have too much of a good thing. One of the big risks with smartphones, games consoles and social media sites is spending too much time online and becoming addicted to using your devices.

To find out where you are on the scale of okay to too much, ask yourself:

* *Do you feel anxious when you can't go online?*
* *Are you fearful that you're missing out on everything when you're not online?*
* *Do you lie about how much time you spend online?*
* *Do you get annoyed if people try to talk to you when you're posting or texting?*
* *Do you obsessively check emails, social media or texts?*

* *Do you become annoyed if people ask you why you're online so much?*
* *Do you get angry to the point of rage when your parents ask you to switch off?*

If any or all of the above ring true and your online life is interfering with your offline life, then you need to ask for help or start to wean yourself off. For example, start with setting times when you can be on tech and times when you have a break. Even if you think it's fine to prioritize what you do online over everything else, bear in mind that being too dependent on tech and living for it is not a good thing. Two hours can rise to four hours and eventually you can find yourself online all the time, from very late at night to first thing in the morning. **A healthy tech attitude is to use tech as part of your life, not to make it all of your life.**

CHAPTER TWO

Texting teens

"What do I text about? Anything. Being bored mostly, or complaining about homework or stupid jokes."

JACK, 13

"It's usually texts about meeting up, where people are and lots of flirting."

SIAN, 13

If you're anything like the average teen, you could be sending as many as 100 texts a day – that's around 3,000 messages a month. That's a lot of texting, IM and a lot of talking and a lot of messaging. On the face of it, what's wrong with messaging all the time?

- *It's cheaper and faster than talking on the phone.*
- *It's fun and entertaining.*
- *You can message lots of friends at once.*
- *It's like being with friends, even when you're at home.*
- *It allows you to express an opinion without being face-to-face.*

For many, it's their main method of communication with friends and, just like emailing or talking on the phone, that's fine. However, what you have to remember is that sending messages to someone is a detached form of communication – even though you're communicating and it feels personal, it's happening from a distance. This means messaging is a very easy way to annoy someone, or upset him or her without meaning to. It's also an easy way to say something innocent that then gets misinterpreted and blown out of proportion.

"One of my friends fell out with me because she said I never added kisses after my comments. Apparently that meant I didn't care about her."

CARI, 12

The problem is, because the person you are texting can't hear your tone of voice or see your expression when they read your texts (a part of how we read people in real life), it's very easy to take a text in the wrong way.

On top of this, because of the distance, when things go wrong it's all too easy to snap back and say something mean, and that's where problems start. Mixed in with all this is text etiquette, which seems to be different in everyone's books.

So consider these questions:

* *Do you answer texts right away or is it acceptable to wait?*
* *Should you add a smiley face when you say something mean?*

* *Can you group text a 'funny' story about someone or is that being horrible?*
* *Should you add kisses or does that mean too much?*
* *Is it rude to ignore someone's text if they're not asking a direct question?*

As you can see, it's all too easy for a text war to break out without you even intending it. If you're wondering where you stand on the texting front, try our quiz to see where your text behaviour might land you.

QUIZ What's your texting style?

1 *When someone sends you a text what do you do?*

a Respond right away
b Wait until you've got time to respond
c Ignore it unless it's from a very good friend

2 *Where are you most likely to text from?*

a Everywhere. You text in lessons, in bed and even in the bathroom. Texting is part of you
b Your bedroom when you're alone
c When you're out and about

3 *What do you think of friends who don't text?*

a They're weird
b They miss out on a lot of fun and stuff
c You don't care

4 *Do you ever use your phone to call someone?*

a Never
b Only your parents as they are the only ones who use phones to call people
c Sometimes

5 *Do you ever flirt by text?*

a Yes, all the time
b Yes, some of the time
c Only if you really like someone

6 *Someone texts you a rude picture – what do you do?*

a Laugh and send it on
b Laugh but feel too embarrassed to send it to more than your best friend
c Laugh and delete it

7 *If someone needs to tell you something important but very private, how should they do it?*

a By text – it's immediate and private
b By email – it's fast and very private
c Face-to-face – it's the most private way

8 *If your parents told you your holiday destination had no signal, how would you feel?*

a In a panic. All these people would be trying to get in touch all the time and think you were ignoring them
b Irritated – how will you speak to your friends?
c A bit worried but not that much

9 *Someone takes your text the wrong way – what do you do?*

- **a** Text them an apology
- **b** Text and talk to them in person
- **c** Talk to them

10 *If you text a friend and he/she doesn't reply, how do you feel?*

- **a** Angry that he/she's ignoring you
- **b** Worried that he/she is annoyed with you
- **c** You're okay, they're probably busy

Mostly As: OTT Texter You love texting so much that you're probably texting as you read this. The phone is as much a part of you as anything else and no matter what happens (or doesn't happen) you're likely to be texting about it to friends, acquaintances and even non-friends. The problem is, because you text A LOT you assume everyone else does too, so you're likely to take offence if you don't get an immediate reply from a friend. Or be annoyed if others don't text you when they say they will. Worst of all, you can't imagine being separated from your phone as it's your number one mode of communication, which means school can be a hassle for you (though we're pretty sure you text secretly in lessons). Friends may also find your constant texting and need to be texted back instantly a little wearing, which means it may be time to wean yourself off texts a little.

TEXT FACT *Research shows that face-to-face time hasn't been diminished by texting. Technology has simply added another layer to how teens communicate.*

Mostly Bs: Text Worrier
You love texting but if you're a little honest, it often makes you feel worried and anxious. You're often afraid your words will be taken the wrong way, and feel concerned about why someone hasn't texted you back or whether you've texted something funny or unfunny. While you love keeping in touch with friends, some friends' OTT texting wears you out. Don't be afraid to take a step back from texting if it isn't fun for you. The key is to text if you feel the need and don't text if you can't be bothered. Plus don't worry about other people's text expectations. Just because they want immediate replies and kisses added – don't feel you have to do it.

Mostly Cs: Text Avoider You don't mind texting but it's not your main method of communication. You love hearing from friends, sharing a joke and even complaining about life via text but you don't live to text. Due to this, some of your friends can feel rebuffed by you. Be sure to let OTT texters know that you're not like them so they don't take offence when you take days to reply, or even forget completely. Bearing that in mind, it does help to be aware of friends' needs. If someone texts something urgent make an effort to respond with the same urgency, whether by text or in person, for the sake of your friendship if nothing else.

Text etiquette

When it comes to texts it's worth bearing in mind that a lot can go wrong. Below are some of the top text mishaps that cause problems in the non-text world.

* *Sending a rude text about someone to the wrong person.*
* *Accidentally sending a text about a friend's behaviour to the friend in question.*
* *Funny and not so funny auto-correct mishaps.*
* *Forgetting you're on a group message and messaging about someone in the group.*

This is why thinking about what you say and how you say it is important. To safeguard yourself, check who you're sending a text to before you send. Then always read back what you've written to see if it sounds as funny as it did when you wrote it. If you're at all unsure, don't press send. Just these simple steps can avoid a text war breaking out.

TEXT FACT *Research by scientists at a US university has found that texting while walking increases your chances of having an accident. From falling off the kerb, to walking into lampposts and being hit by a car.*

Text etiquette also includes how and when you respond to a friend. Texting right away isn't always possible, so if you're in the middle of a text conversation and you have to go, make sure you tell the person you'll get back to him/her later. Likewise if someone sends you an urgent text don't ignore it, respond with the urgency they need.

Remember, not all texts are urgent so don't feel under pressure to keep texting (even if you have an OTT friend as a texter). Again tell them you're signing off and they won't be offended.

Emoticons, acronyms and kisses

Where you stand on this subject is personal. Some people love littering their texts with sad and smiley faces, LOL, AITR (adult in the room) and xxxx. Others can't stand it. The problem with these symbols is that people often use them to hide the fact they are saying something mean. So when you get upset they can say, 'I was only joking. Didn't you see the smiley face?' If you use them, make sure you don't use them to hide the fact you're being angry, aggressive or mean. If you have a problem with someone it's always better to say it face-to-face than by text. Also make sure you know what you're saying. A common mistake is to think that LOL means Lots of Love, when in fact it means Laugh Out Loud.

Would you say it in real life?

Lastly think about what you're writing. When texting it's very easy to get carried away and just text and text and text! Before you hit send, always think: 'Would I say this face-to-face?' If you wouldn't, don't text it. Be wary of spreading gossip, or slander. You may think you're having a laugh or simply being funny, but texts have a long life and they also count as evidence if someone feels you are bullying them.

Flirting by text

"I flirt all the time by text. It's fun, it doesn't always mean anything"

MJ, 13

Let's face, it everyone (even adults) flirts by text. Why? Well because it's a 'safe' way to say what you're thinking without having to risk being rejected, laughed at or seen by others. It also means that you don't have to do embarrassing face-to-face flirting and can afford to sit back and think before you reply. This means you can prove to someone that you're not only attractive but funny too. If you're keen to text-flirt in the right way, here are some Do's and Don'ts to help.

1 **Do be clear about your intentions.** Are you being serious or just joking around? If you're joking around, don't lead the person on for a laugh. Not only is this hurtful but it will backfire big time once word gets around that you can't be trusted. In the same way, if you want him/her to call you or date you, make sure you say that in your text and be clear. Otherwise you can flirt and feel as if you've been 100% clear but the other person may not realize it and you'll end up feeling rejected when you actually haven't been.

2 **Don't be too revealing in your texts.** Especially if you don't really know the person you're flirting with. The question to ask yourself is can you trust them? That's trust them not to share your messages, trust them not to make fun of you and trust them to take you seriously. If you're at all unsure stick to light-hearted text flirting until you're more sure.

3 **Don't be rude or too OTT.** Again this is an area that can easily put people off. You may think you're being funny or that's what guys or girls want to hear, but the reality is we are all different. Something your friends think is funny and flirty may not be interpreted that way. This especially goes for pictures and jokes.

4 **Don't play games by text.** Having a flirting match and then making him or her wait for a reply just sends the message that you're not interested. Likewise, sending a mis-text just to make the other person jealous screams needy. Game-playing by text is not flirting and does not send a message that you like the person in question.

5 **Do be aware that girls and guys text flirt differently.** Guys tend to joke around and be a bit rude, girls tend to hold back and be a bit mysterious about what they want. This means that over-analyzing what's being texted with friends (while fun) isn't going to make things clearer. If you're unsure what a text means, ask the person in question.

6 **Don't go overboard with acronyms and emoticons (smiley/sad faces).** Things like 'ROFL' (roll on the floor laughing), 'MTFBWU' (may the force be

with you) or overzealous 'LOL' usage should be reserved for texts with BFF not people you're flirting with.

7 **Do appropriate flirting.** Are you flirting with someone who is single, appropriate for you age-wise and that you have actually met in person? If not, stop flirting right now as you're in dangerous territory.

8 **Don't read too much into texts.** Sometimes we assume we are being flirted with by text when we're not. This is because some people do not follow the steps above and there are even some people who just can't help flirting in all their texts. If you feel you are reading too much into a text conversation, or the person in question doesn't mirror his or her text behaviour when you're face-to-face, step back and try to read the words as they are, without attaching extra meaning to them.

Finally, if someone keeps text flirting when you don't want them to, there are a number of ways to handle it:

* *Refuse to flirt back – be normal with your responses.*
* *Tell them you're in a relationship and you don't want to be flirted with.*
* *If they won't listen to you when you try the two options above, simply refuse to answer their texts.*

Instant messaging

"I have 100 friends on my list and sometimes I'll talk to 10 at one time, usually 3 or 4."
HARRY, 13

Figures from the Pew Internet & American Life Project show that 74% of teens use instant messaging. **While most instant messages are harmless, more than a third of teens say they use IM to say things they don't want to say in face-to-face conversations with their peers.** Almost a fifth (17%) have used IM to ask someone out and more than a tenth (13%) have used IM to break up with someone.

That's the problem with instant messaging – it's so, well, instant. That sounds ridiculous but it means that when you message something in anger, when you're tired or when you're just generally irritated you can upset friends, turn them against you and make something innocent into a big deal. Again this is because IM is indirect

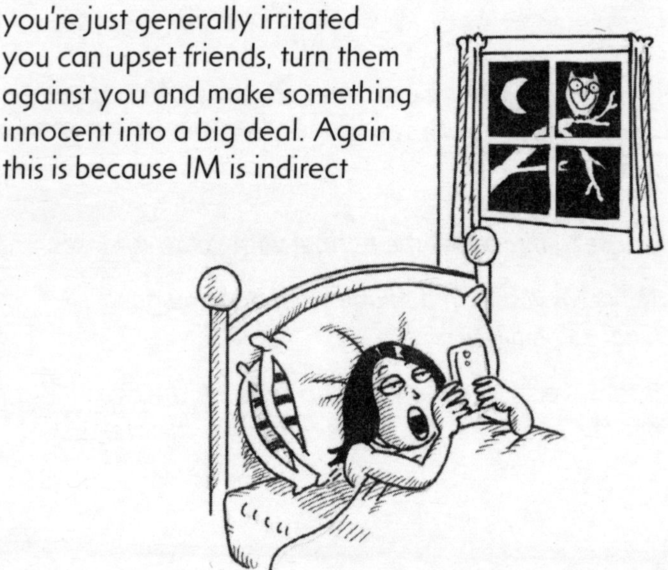

communication so your friends can't tell if you're being funny or writing something with a smile on your face.

The other problem with IM (which maybe your parents feel is more of a problem than you do) is that it can be addictive. You can find yourself messaging at all hours and on a constant basis. Plus if you feel your social status is based on the number of friends you have, you can feel pressurized to accept requests from people you don't know. This then means you're sharing information with a whole range of people that you can't wholly trust.

Then there are people who use other people's accounts or fake accounts to disguise their identity in conversations with others. This can lead on to feelings of being bullied and harassed. If this happens, you need to tell someone what's happening and sign off for a while.

The best way to deal with all of the above is to:

* *Only befriend people on IM that you know.*
* *Be careful what and how you say things (if you wouldn't say it in person, don't say it via IM).*
* *Don't overdo it – constantly getting IM from friends can be really annoying.*

Text bullying

Text bullying is on the rise. If you're unsure of what this is, it means **sending mean, embarrassing, untrue or threatening messages to or about someone by text**. In many ways it can be more damaging than face-to-face bullying (though the two things tend to go hand-in-hand). This is because it can happen 24 hours a day, so it can feel inescapable. Unfortunately, due to the nature of texts, text bullies are much meaner because they don't have to see their victims' faces when they do it, and because they can often do it anonymously.

If you're using texts to bully, or know someone who is, it's important to realize that text bullying can be traced and you can face criminal charges.

If it's happening to you, it's important to:

1 Keep the texts as evidence.

2 Tell someone what's happening to you. Even if you have to give your phone to that person so you aren't being harassed.

Text bullying includes:

* *Being sent abusive, rude and threatening texts.*
* *Being sent abusive, violent and hardcore pictures or videos (see Sexting page 36).*
* *Being harassed by texts (whether there is a message or not) 24/7.*
* *Being threatened by people anonymously.*
* *Receiving group texts where people say nasty things about you.*
* *Someone sending a text you sent in private to a group of people.*

There are some ways to stop text bullying. These include the options below:

* *Get another SIM card or change your mobile number.*
* *Once you have a new phone number, only give it out to members of your family and close friends and make sure they do not give it to anyone.*

Sexting

"I liked this guy till he started to send me dodgy pictures of himself. My mum saw one and went mad."

G.S, 13

"My friends all send porn stuff to each other. Some of it's gross but that's quite funny."

SAM, 13

"I let him take this video of me on my phone that I now really regret, but I didn't realize he had sent himself a copy. His mate says he's sharing it as I dumped him. I'm really worried."

ALI, 14

Sexting is a term used to describe a range of activities that people do on their phones, from sharing sexy images or videos to sending porn, or posting sexually suggestive messages on social networks. Sexting also includes forwarding sexual photos and videos of under 18s (which is breaking the law). This can be by text, instant messaging or email, or on social networks.

While it's normal for teens to be interested in the idea of sex and relationships, it's the ease with which everyone can now access pornographic material, and take and send photos, that has led to sexting.

Teens often feel pressurized into taking and passing on provocative images because they're told 'it's just a bit of fun', or 'everyone is doing it'. The images themselves can be anything from nudity to partial exposure, or something very suggestive. Girls in particular say they feel pressured to have suggestive images taken to 'fit in' with friends or please boyfriends. While boys admit that they feel pressurized to pass the images on.

We all do things when we want people to like us, to impress friends or because we think we're doing them for love. But one thing to think long and hard about is allowing someone to have naked, semi-naked or provocative pictures of you. Someone may say they will never show the pictures to anyone, or that you'd do it if you loved/liked/fancied them or that everyone is doing it, but the reality is – once you send a picture, anything can happen to it. Images can be copied, posted on a social media site, used to bribe you to do something or simply passed around without you knowing. **As with any kind of peer or relationship pressure, bear in mind the following:**

* *Anyone who truly cares about you won't pressurize you to do something you don't want to.*
* *Not everyone is sending round pictures of themselves.*
* *You can never trust anyone 100% with naked pictures.*

As for how to say no – sometimes the best way to turn down someone's requests for pictures is a firm 'no', followed up by, 'I don't feel comfortable/happy doing that'. If they put further pressure on you after that, it just shows that the points above are all true.

If you have been sent something explicit and are being urged by friends to send it on, always bear in mind that you could be breaking the law if you have in your possession, or distribute indecent images of, a person under the age of 18 to someone else. Even if the image is not of someone under 18, think before you send it. Over a third of under 18s say they have received an offensive or distressing sexual image by text or email.

Think:

* *Is the image of someone you know? How would they feel about it being passed on?*
* *Would the person you're sending it to be offended?*
* *How would you feel if the image was of you?*

If someone is sending images of you, or sending you upsetting images or messages, don't be afraid to tell your parents and report it. You may be worried about the reaction of your parents but what's happening is a form of bullying. And if you're being persuaded to have naked images taken you also need to speak up and seek help (see help section for more details).

So why do people 'sext'?

1. *Curiosity is the number one reason. Many teens are curious about sex, which leads to exploration and is the reason why images are sent around.*
2. *Low self-esteem – trying to show you're attractive or that you're popular can lead people to take and send images and keep photos.*

3. *Love – people do all kinds of things in the name of love. You might think you're going to be in love forever or that your partner is 100% trustworthy. Sadly this isn't the case with most people. Teens fall in and out of love all the time and being dumped can lead people to do all kinds of nasty things – like send your pictures to others.*

4. *Peer pressure – maybe you think everyone is doing it, or that you'll be seen as 'immature' if you don't let someone you like take your photo.*

The problem with letting images of yourself be taken is that once they are out there, you can't control who sees them or where the images go. There's no way of knowing how many people have saved, tagged and shared them. This is why you need to tell someone what's happening right away. Forget feeling embarrassed or getting into trouble – nip the problem in the bud so it doesn't get out of hand.

SEXTING FACTS

38% of 13–18 year olds have received a sexually explicit message.
39% admit sharing intimate images.
40% do not see anything wrong with sending topless images.
70% knew the sender; the majority were peers or current girlfriends or boyfriends. A small minority were from known adults.

'Survey conducted by 'South West Grid for Learning' (SWGfL) & University of Plymouth over 500 1318 year olds

If it's one person who has an inappropriate image of you, ask them to delete it on all their devices and if they won't, speak up and ask for help. If the image been posted to social networks, like Facebook, Tumblr and Instagram, it can be hard to know where the image has gone and who has got it. You can contact and report what's happened to a social network site to request removal of content. Your request needs to show that it breaks the site's terms and conditions.

CHAPTER THREE

Social media

"I'm on Facebook, Instagram and Tumblr – pretty much every day. What do me and my friends do? The usual – post funny pictures, talk, send videos – the same as everyone else."

JACK, 13

Who doesn't love social media? There are a few people out there who don't embrace it, but on the whole the figures are staggering. 81% of teens aged 12 – 17 say they use social media sites, with Facebook being the most heavily used site with 94% of teens saying they have a profile there.

Twitter is used by a quarter of teens and Instagram is very close behind. On top of this are a wealth of other social media sites, such as Tumblr, YouTube, Google+, and the lesser-known ones (well lesser known to adults but well known by teens) such as Vine, Pheed and Snapchat. In fact by the time you read this, no doubt more social media sites and apps will have sprung up. Some will last the distance and others will fall out of favour, but whatever you use, the fact is social media is here to stay.

For those who don't yet know, a social network like Facebook is a way of staying in touch and making new connections with friends, family, famous people and even people you don't know (like friends of friends). The way each network works is slightly different (read on for more on each network) but once you add 'friends' you can talk online, share photos and videos, send private messages, chat with groups of people, give your view on everything from films to foods you like, and play games.

Below is a well-known example that explains the difference between a few social media sites, using doughnuts as an example. Take a look to help you understand how some networks work.

Twitter « I am eating a doughnut »

Facebook « I like doughnuts »

Instagram « Here is a vintage-looking picture of my doughnut »

YouTube « Watch me eat a doughnut »

Tumblr « Here's lots of pictures of doughnuts I like »

Pinterest « Here are recipes, pictures and pretty stuff about doughnuts »

What are you doing on social media?

"Often it's all about who can post the best picture and get the most 'likes'."

ANNA, 13

Social media means you can pretty much communicate in any way you want, with any type of media (photos, videos, live streaming), but this means there is a lot of space for things to go wrong. Things like becoming friends with people you ultimately don't know, online bullying, saying, doing or posting the wrong things, upsetting friends, and basically feeling left out and rejected. In fact, anything you can feel in real life you can feel online, and sometimes it feels worse online because:

1. *Everyone is looking.*
2. *You tend to be on your own so it feels 10 times worse.*
3. *Online content has a long life span. Embarrassing pictures can feel as if they never go away and something you say can easily be repeated and brought up time and time again.*

Social networking is a very public space, which means that although you may think you're just talking to your best friends, in reality (depending on the network you are using and your privacy settings) what you're posting could be going out to friends of friends of friends, i.e. complete strangers. The other hidden danger is that there are many dubious people on social media sites. They do everything from pretending to be something they're not, to posting explicit and sometimes illegal images (see the dangers of online pornography on page 89). This all means that you need to be doubly careful about who you friend, what information you give out and how much you believe (for more on this see Chapter 4 on privacy).

SOCIAL MEDIA FACT: *A third of teens are friends on social media with people they have never met.*

*Pew Internet & American Life Project

Having said that, social media is worth getting to grips with because it is fun and it is part of everyday life whether you love it or not. Most of the people you know use it to communicate, so it's worth considering what you're saying, who's reading it and what's happening on the networks you're using. If you're keen to get to grips with it here's what you need to know.

What are the social media sites?

Unless you have been living on a desert island, it's likely that you've heard of Facebook and Twitter and probably Instagram and Tumblr. However, there are a huge amount of social networking sites and apps that appear monthly, if not weekly, so here's what you need to know about some of the most popular.

Facebook

Most people know what Facebook is. It's the biggest and most well-known social networking site in the world. Facebook has so many users that if it were a country it would be the third biggest in the world.

FACEBOOK FACTS

There are over a billion active users, of which about 9% are fake accounts. Plus despite age restrictions (you can't join Facebook if you're under 13) there are around 12 million under 13s active on the site.

The problem with Facebook is that many people are so concerned with having a large number of friends that they friend anyone who asks. This means that a huge number of people you don't know not only have access to your pictures and postings, but your personal details as well. On top of this, research shows that many teens don't think about privacy, which means postings and pictures can go to a much wider audience than you might imagine.

YouTube

54% of all teens are on YouTube, and it's the world's second largest search engine after Google – that's a whole lot of video watching and uploading. Most of the things people do on YouTube are funny, clever and smart. There are great videos to watch and share, but again some content is inevitably violent and offensive. You need to be careful what you share, what you comment on, what you search for and who you are talking to.

Twitter

This site allows users to send text-based messages of up to 140 characters, known as tweets. You can also tweet pictures and videos, join in trending chat topics and start your own. You can follow whoever you want, but people cannot DM (direct message) you unless you agree to be friends with them.

TWITTER FACT

60% of teens said their tweets were public and 12% didn't know whether they were public or not.

*Pew Internet & American Life Project

The problem here is privacy. Many people attempt to get as many followers as possible and so accept anyone as friends. By doing this they put themselves at risk of being direct messaged by a stranger.

Tumblr

This is a micro-blogging social networking platform where users post videos, images and short posts. Most of the people on Tumblr are aged 14–25 and the site boasts 108.4 million blogs with 60 million posts. It's a fun site but again, as you can post anything, there are some seriously explicit blogs that are worth avoiding.

Kik

This is a smartphone messenger system that allows you to exchange videos, smiley faces and more. As a private messaging system it is hard to monitor and easily exploited, as it can be used on any smartphone, iPod touch or tablet. Some people blatantly use Kik to send and receive nude pictures (see sexting in Chapter 2).

Instagram

This photo-sharing app allows users to upload a photo from their smartphone library, or take a photo and use Instagram to change the way it looks. The user can upload the photo to any social networks synced to their Instagram account. At the same time, it is uploaded to the Instagram community where people can like and comment on it.

The single most important thing to realize is that, by default, anyone can view these photos. In other words, your profile and your photos are publicly viewable unless you tell Instagram otherwise. This means that someone (or rather, anyone at all) can like your photo, start talking to you and ask to add you as a friend, say on Kik or somewhere else that, unlike Instagram, is private.

The only way to safeguard yourself is to:

* *Set privacy settings on Instagram so only those allowed can see your pictures.*
* *Turn off geotagging/location-based services for Instagram.*
* *Do not put your Kik Messenger username in your Instagram profiles or picture messages asking people to 'Kik you at…'.*

Vine

Vine lets you record and share six-second video clips on an endless loop. Pornography was a big problem for Vine, but they have since taken action by removing as much of the explicit content as they could. Users can now only browse appropriate hashtags, and if you do search for a porn-related hashtag, there won't be any results.

Pheed

This is a social media platform that lets you share text, photos, videos and audio. It's one of the biggest networks for teenage users, with 81% between the ages of 14 and 25. Posts are limited to 240 characters and, unlike other networking sites, users can put their content behind a paywall. This means that only your friends can see your content and you can watermark content, which means you own it and people can't share it without your permission.

Snapchat

This is a photo-sharing app for sending photos and videos that appear and then disappear. It's a huge hit with a lot of people because it's simple, it's secret and it feels like fun.

If you use Snapchat to send funny pictures or even rude ones, it's worth remembering that just because it disappears doesn't mean it's gone. There is a way to restore deleted Snapchat pictures on some phones and tablets. It's also possible to capture a screenshot of what's being sent or to take a picture of the picture with another camera. As a result be careful what you send, even for a joke.

SnapKidz is the new iOS version of Snapchat where kids under the age of 13 can use the app but they won't actually be able to send photos.

Ask.fm

This is a social media site used mainly by tweens and teens, where users can ask other users simple questions, and responses are limited to 300 characters. The questions can be from a named user, or (and this is the dangerous part) completely anonymously asked. Ask.fm has no parental controls and, though it seems harmless, it has become known for its bullying threads and even 'slut shaming' (see Chapter 5 for more on this) due to its anonymous nature. Many people have been harassed and driven to despair by some of the horrible things being written anonymously when they ask what seems like quite an innocent question.

Skype

Skype is a free video chat and messaging service that many kids use to chat to their friends. Like any social network, Skype can be used inappropriately. In particular the chat feature can be used to 'groom' or cyberbully and the video feature can be used to post explicit and/or illegal images. For this reason, never post an address or home phone number on a Skype profile and don't accept a request from anyone you don't know. Even if they say they know you or your family.

Omegle

This is a free online chat website that allows users to communicate with strangers without registering. The service randomly pairs users in one-to-one chat sessions based on interests. They chat or video chat anonymously using the handles 'You' and 'Stranger'. Omegle contains a disclaimer that states that no one under the age of 13 may use Omegle, and no one under the age of 18 may use it without parents' permission. Participants' IP addresses are stored for up to 120 days.

Keek
This is best described as a video-sharing app version of Instagram. It launched in 2013 and received 250 million page views and 21 million visits in its first month alone. Keek allows users to share short videos with their friends.

The problems of social media and being social

"There is no problem with social media. It's the people who use it that are a problem."

MAX, 14

Max's comment above is true to some extent – it's certain people on social media who make it a problem, just as they do in life. However, it's also worth understanding that the way these social networks work is problematic, too.

For a start, the sites are now all interconnected. You can sign up for many, such as Ask.fm, via your Twitter and Facebook account (a way to avoid having to key in all your information again). But every time you do this, you're allowing the site you're joining not only to access all the information you have on Facebook, but also to post on your behalf on Facebook (do you want them to have access to everything?). For instance, if you sign up via Facebook to use the scrapbook site Pinterest, every picture you pin there will appear on your Facebook profile, too.

Social media sites by their very nature also encourage you to share way more than you would in everyday life. Think of it this way – if you were feeling sad and upset would you instantly tell everyone in your school? Or if you were angry with a friend would you stand on the school stage and have a fight in front of everyone? Or if you found an explicit but funny picture would you send it to everyone you knew? The answer is probably no, but this is what happens on social networking sites all the time and why simple things become problematic.

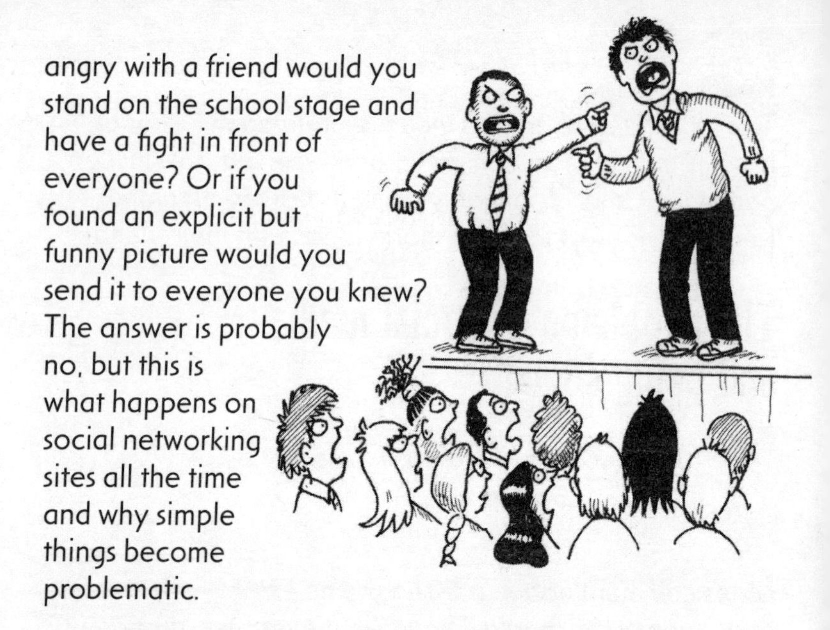

Here are some other ways networking can go wrong:

Potential problem one
We post quickly without thinking. So, we don't pause and consider whether or not we should say something to everyone we know before we make it public.

Potential problem two
We follow or have so many friends that we often forget we're actually talking about someone who's connected to us in some way (via a friend of a friend).

Potential problem three
We share things (like our views, pictures and videos) that are offensive to others. It's worth bearing in mind that the settings on sites like Facebook change all the time. Which means if you currently 'like' an offensive picture on

someone else's page it can get transferred to your timeline and all your friends will see it.

Potential problem four
You go on your friends' timelines and comment as them. This is often a joke but it can cause untold problems, especially if your friends' parents are watching.

Potential problem five
You engage with too many people you don't know, sharing too much information and getting too close to them. Remember profiles can be fake and people are often not who they say they are.

Potential problem six Your accounts are all synced – so what appears on one site, instantly appears on another that may not have the same privacy settings.

What are you posting?

"I post about what I am doing mostly and selfies and stuff my friends and I like."

BRITNEY, 12

"I post pictures and rude jokes."

LUKE, 12

"I post videos and pictures and sometimes naked stuff. People are lying if they say they don't do that."

MAX, 14

So what are you posting? In the main it's likely to be the stuff you chat about in person, the things you like, rubbish homework, being bored and whole lot of other stuff that you don't give much thought to. Whatever you post, the important question to always ask yourself is would you say what you're posting to someone's face? Often with social media there is a disconnect between what we say (our words) and the impact on the people reading it. So we all too readily express our anger, disappointment or bad-taste humour in a way that's not appropriate. Doing things we wouldn't do in real life, but will do online.

INAPPROPRIATE PICTURES FACT *54% of Snapchat users have received an 'inappropriate picture' during use of the app, while 61% of these said that they'd received images of 'inappropriate poses or gestures'; 47% had received nude pictures and a further 11% claimed to have seen images of 'criminal acts'.*

The same goes for sending videos and pictures. A lot of what is posted is sent for a laugh, but you always need to consider:

A *If what you're sending is legal (naked pictures of under 16s is not legal).*

B *How offensive it is?*

Many adults get this wrong too, posting horrible pictures for everyone to see because they think they are funny.

It's also worth bearing in mind that the pictures and posts you send about the causes you believe in may be offensive. Many groups and pages (especially animal rights pages) use shock tactics to get people to take notice on social media. A lot of these pictures are very graphic and upsetting, and many people on your timeline will not want to see them.

Always think about whether you're sharing too much. By all means share away about yourself within reason, but consider if you are saying too much about your innermost feelings. Sometimes it can be easy to sit down and write about how you're feeling, but once it's out there you can't take it back (even if you delete it). If you feel the need to express a problem, anger or worry, think about emailing or private messaging over posting.

When it comes to sharing about family and friends, remember that people are entitled to their privacy – even if they are related to you or in a picture with you. Also think about what you are unintentionally sharing when you post. For example, the hashtags *#homework* or *#homealone* might be meant for your friends, but they will also let everyone know your age and that you are home unsupervised.

Be considerate with your comments. Again this is about being appropriate. Funny comments don't work if someone is upset, being serious or looking for a shoulder to cry on. Think before commenting on people's photographs. Many photos posted online are tagged, so if you make a critical comment about how someone looks it will get back to them.

Finally don't be obsessed with the 'Like' competition. Too many people are fixated by the number of 'likes' they have for posts and pictures, and how many friends they can collect. Social media does feel like a popularity contest at times, but it's not. People who tend to have in excess of 600 friends and have zillions of likes on everything they say, tend to be people who are on social media ALL the time, talking to people they don't know ALL the time.

Mean behaviour on social networking sites

"There's lots of nastiness that goes on online. I've had people put horrible pictures up of me and then had all these people comment on how ugly I am. It's really hurtful and no one ever forgets."

HAYLEY, 14

We all know cyberbullying is on the rise (for more on this see Chapter 5). Bullying through social media was recently described by the *Sunday Times* as being 'epidemic' and it is. For many people, social media sites, such as Facebook and Instagram, and anonymous messaging sites and apps have also become tools that can be used to intimidate, harass, bully and be mean to others.

Consider if you do, or have seen or experienced, any of the following:

* *Posting horrible photos or videos of 'friends' on Facebook and other sites and then tagging all friends so that everyone sees them.*

* *Posting mean messages or 'jokes' about someone anonymously.*
* *Posting comments that are double-edged, for example, 'Those shoes are so different!' – which could be taken as a compliment or an insult.*
* *Bombarding someone's timeline with horrible comments.*
* *Group messaging a joke about someone.*
* *Spreading gossip and slander about someone.*
* *Being exclusive about your postings (posting pictures and posts to let other friends know they haven't been included).*

When using social media the most important thing to bear in mind is: 'How would I feel if someone posted this about me?' Stop and think, and if you're in any doubt don't post it. Even acts that seem harmless at the time, such as posting a funny picture of a friend, can become upsetting if everyone joins in with writing comments and sharing the picture. Your friend may not mind you laughing at the pic, but she might if the whole world starts laughing too.

CHAPTER FOUR

Privacy issues

"I'm not bothered with privacy controls. I've got nothing to hide and I don't do stupid stuff online."

CAM, 14

Studies and surveys show that when it comes to privacy online, teens have a lower concern for it than adults, with less than 10% worrying about it. This doesn't mean teens don't bother with privacy, but simply that they worry less about who's seeing and sharing their content. If this is you, it's likely that you don't see the possible implications of giving away large amounts of personal information, and also because it just feels normal to share everything with everyone.

However, it's very important to think about who is looking and commenting on your content. While many under 18s say their profiles are set to private and only visible to 'friends', a fifth of teens still leave their profiles set to public so everyone can see everything (Pew Internet & American Life Project). Of those who are on the friends setting, a third readily admit they don't actually know all their 'friends'. This means that they aren't sure who's doing what with their comments and pictures.

Whether you think about it or not, privacy is a very valuable asset in life. Contrary to what many people believe, privacy online is not just about protecting yourself from the dangers of the online world (bullying and predators), but also protecting yourself from yourself. This may sound strange but learning to keep some things private, like your innermost feelings, embarrassing pictures, family matters and so on, allows you to keep your mistakes and family issues under wraps. Spill it to the whole world online and it will never go away.

FACT *57% of teens say they have decided not to post something online because they were concerned it would reflect badly on them in the future.*

*Pew Internet & American Life Project

One way to think about this subject is to imagine writing a personal diary. Would you ever leave this in the school library for everyone to read? No, of course you wouldn't because it's private – and yet many people treat social media as their personal diary, writing things that expose their personal world to others.

The same goes for posting embarrassing or rude pictures and stories. They are funny for a moment, but not so funny when a prospective employer Googles you further down the line. While this might sound like a far-off future issue, it is already affecting whether some students get the university and college places they want, so it is worth considering.

For this reason it's worth thinking about the impact of your digital footprint and how content (pictures, videos and written posts) associated with your name may affect your reputation both right now and in the future.

QuiZ How private are you?

1 *You and your best friend fall out. You feel really angry and resentful about something he/she has done to you. What do you do?*

- **a** Immediately post how betrayed you feel online, being sure to name who you're talking about
- **b** Post that you're furious and wait for comments before saying why
- **c** Have a text war with them

2 *You take a really bad picture of your sister that makes you laugh. She asks you to delete it but you...*

- **a** Post it online and tag her so her friends can see it
- **b** Put it on Instagram because you're not connected to her on that
- **c** Message it to a few friends

3 *A really disgusting video is doing the rounds. Friends ask you to share it on your timeline. What do you do?*

- **a** Share it because everyone else is
- **b** Share it but not on Facebook
- **c** Don't share it

4 *You're home alone and feeling upset. What are you most likely to do?*

- **a** See if anyone's around to chat online
- **b** Post a message about it
- **c** Text a friend

5 *How many of your online friends do you know well in the real world?*

- **a** At least half of them
- **b** Most of them but many are friends of friends
- **c** Three quarters to all of them

6 *Do you worry that what you say and do online stays there forever?*

- **a** No
- **b** Sometimes
- **c** Often

7 *You hear a great rumour that's both outrageous and funny – what do you do?*

- **a** Post it on Facebook/Twitter
- **b** Message all your friends about it
- **c** Text a few friends

8 *How many friends know your password to social media sites?*

- **a** Loads of them and you know theirs
- **b** Only your best friends
- **c** One friend or no friends

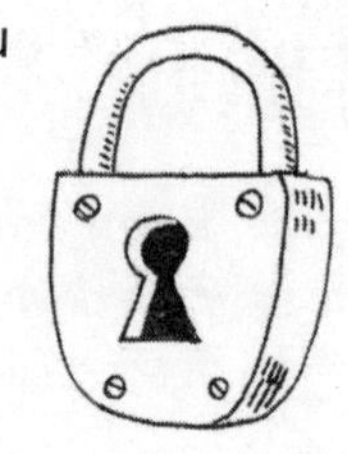

Mostly As You're not private at all and you give very little thought to online privacy. Part of your reasoning could be – why bother because who's looking? The fact is, a lot of people are looking and whether you like it or not, or all your posts build up a picture of who you are to others (that's both the people who know you, and those who don't). This means that if you engage in a lot of gossip and slander, or post rude stuff, it not only gets around but also stays online to haunt you. **Be more careful.**

Mostly Bs You think you're protecting your privacy but in reality you're not. Telling just a few people your password or posting on smaller social networks is still like posting to the world. The fact is, most social networking sites are connected so even though you may think you're not speaking to everyone, the chances are you are. Check the privacy settings you have in place on all social networks, but at the same time check yourself so that you aren't laid open to being exposed when you don't want to be.

Mostly Cs You're cautious and smart about privacy, knowing when to post and when to hold back. It's a good place to be because it means you're not afraid of the online world, simply careful about how you behave there. Well done, you're doing well.

The purpose of privacy controls

"When you sign up for these sites you have to give them all your information – does this mean others can see it too?" **MARK, 12**

Studies show that teens, more than any other age group, are likely to share a wide range of information about themselves on social media. And what's more, as social media sites are designed to encourage the sharing of information and the expansion of friendship networks, this information goes a long, long way (and a lot further than most people think).

Here's what teens share:

92% post their real name

91% post a photo of themselves

84% post their interests, such as movies, music, etc.

82% post their birth date

71% post their school name

71% post the city or town where they live

62% post their relationship status

53% post their email address

24% post videos of themselves

20% post their mobile phone number

*Teens, Social Media and Privacy
http://pewinternet.org/Reports/2013/Teens-Social-Media-And-Privacy.aspx

You may think all these things are fine to share or that everyone shares them but, if you think about it, a lot of the information we've just mentioned makes it very easy to identify you and even find you, which is why you should at least think about setting filters.

Remember, sites always ask for more information than they need when creating your profile, and you don't have to fill it all in. A good way is to fill in the required information, then fill in the rest when you know more about how the site works and your privacy settings.

WHO ARE YOU CONNECTED TO?
98% of Facebook-using teens are friends with people they know from school.
91% of teen Facebook users are friends with members of their extended family.
89% are connected to friends who do not attend the same school.
33% are Facebook friends with other people they have not met in person.

*Pew Internet & American Life Project

Controls are on sites for good reasons, but many of us don't activate them – either because the policies change so often so we can't keep up, or because we can't be bothered and mainly because we want to share. However, listing your name and phone number means that literally anyone connected to you (and that includes friends of friends, i.e. strangers) can text or call you. Listing your school and posting about your activities there means that people can tell where you are and what you're doing. Enabling location services (more on this on page 70) means that people can literally follow you around town.

Usernames and passwords

In this age of constantly having to create passwords and usernames, we're all guilty of either replicating the same one over and over, or choosing something so easy that even a stranger could guess it. If you're keen to stop 'friends' accessing your account pages, and keen to avoid being hacked by people who have nothing better to do, it pays to be smart about passwords and usernames.

While you may want to pay homage to your favourite celeb or band, it never pays to use them as a password. Or your pet's name, or your nickname. Likewise, be careful about the username you choose for yourself. It may sound funny when you're concocting it, but it gives an impression of you online. For instance, calling yourself 'nipples36' or 'bloodbath14' isn't the image you really want to portray.

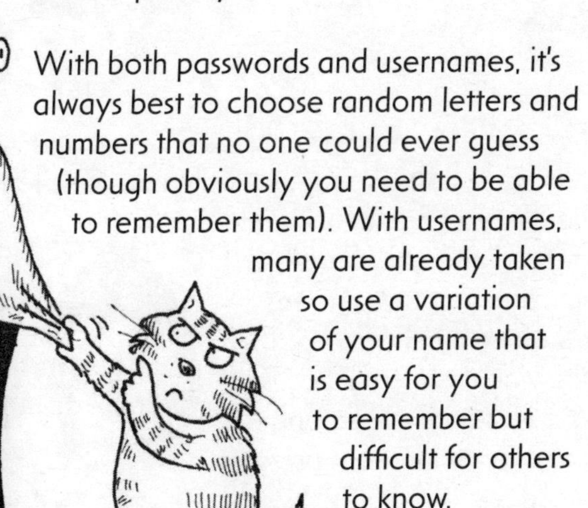

With both passwords and usernames, it's always best to choose random letters and numbers that no one could ever guess (though obviously you need to be able to remember them). With usernames, many are already taken so use a variation of your name that is easy for you to remember but difficult for others to know.

Try your middle name, or mix your names together, or spell your name backwards, or call yourself a name that you like and no one else knows.

For a strong password make sure it:

* *Is at least eight characters long.*
* *Does not contain your username, real name, or pet's name.*
* *Does not contain a word.*
* *Is different from other passwords.*

Always keep your passwords secret

"I'd say about five of my friends know my password. It's okay, I trust them. I know their passwords too, so if they ever did anything I'd do something back."

JULES, 14

If you've ever read someone's timeline and wondered why they were being so rude or ridiculously out of character, the chances are it's a friend pretending to be them. An amazing amount of teens tell others their passwords, allowing them easy access to their social media pages and everything from private messages to pictures.

If you've ever shared your password, it was probably because you wanted to show you trust your friends or because you really, really liked someone. The bad news is, sharing passwords can lead to all kinds of nasty problems.

Firstly, we rarely stay friends with someone forever, which means we fall out, have disputes and sometimes get nasty with each other. When this happens, a fight can move online and when passwords are known, fake posts can appear – posts that are both vindictive and destructive.

PRIVACY FACTS *30% of online teens report sharing their passwords with a friend, boyfriend or girlfriend. 47% of girls and 27% of boys aged 14-17 say they have shared their password.*

Secondly, people are nosy and if you give them the key to your pages and accounts they can snoop into your private messages, see who you're connected to and basically get inside your head. If you're okay with that, go ahead and give it out, but if you'd like to retain your privacy keep that password secret.

Be careful of over sharing

"I know it's a bad idea to post revealing content. I've seen what happens to friends who do. One posted he was getting drunk after school in the fields – the teachers and his parents saw it and went mad."

TOM, 13

The very best kind of privacy control is in your head. Thinking before you post, comment or tag or send can save you a whole load of hassle. The rule is if you feel unsure about whether or not to post something, don't do it.

This is very true when it comes to boasting about stupid deeds (see quote on page 65) and about things that possibly or definitely break the law. One 21 year old on Twitter boasted about knocking a cyclist over when driving and then not stopping. Unfortunately for her (and fortunately for everyone else on the road) both the cyclist and the police saw her tweet and she was arrested.

It's also true of your feelings. On the spur of the moment it's easy to feel angry and furious and post something, or feel sad and say something dramatic that you don't mean. Ten minutes later you may be okay, but your comment will stay up all day and maybe even all week, with people commenting and making a drama out of it for weeks to come. You may like the initial attention, but after a while it gets wearing and then boring.

The reality is, while social networks are great for venting, sharing and relieving the boredom of say, homework, they are not the places to over share. This includes sharing information you know about other people like your family and closest friends. Try to be aware of this when you comment as well as post, because it's all too easy to forget you are not talking one-to-one and that everyone can see what you're saying.

Understand the networks you use

"My friend posted this nasty picture of me from Year 5. I hated it and she said she deleted it but people keep commenting on it and it keeps appearing everywhere."

LIZ, 13

While websites are continually changing, it pays to know how they work (see Chapter 3 for more on this) because this in turn helps you to protect yourself. For instance, if you post a lot of pictures of yourself on Facebook and there is one you'd rather forget, all you need is for one friend to comment on it again (easily done by going through your pictures) and then it goes back to the top of your Facebook feed and becomes news again.

Having said that, Facebook has the strongest privacy controls of all the social networks – you just have to be bothered to use them. If you don't want an update to go to everyone, you have the choice to select who sees it and who doesn't via blocking.

On Instagram, when you sign up you can agree to sync your account to other social networks. This means that when you upload a photo it goes straight to these sites and is also uploaded to the Instagram community where people can like it and comment on it. Anyone can then view these photos unless you tell Instagram otherwise.

With Twitter, all accounts are set up to be public. That means your Twitter posts are visible to anyone who has access to the Internet. All they need to do is go on Twitter and search for you or Google your tweets. You can configure your Twitter account to protect your profile so you approve all new followers, and your updates are only visible to those followers, but the reality is most people don't do this or know they should do this.

If you can face it, always try to find out how an app or site works and what the privacy settings do and don't do before you sign up, so you know what you're letting yourself in for. Or else you can search online for an abridged version that basically tells you what you need to know and why.

It is always worth searching YouTube to see how sites work and for safety advice. There are some very good videos that can help you stay informed and in control, especially when new privacy updates come into being. Like anything, stick to known and trusted sources for this information.

The rise of social messaging apps

"I prefer being on WhatsApp – my friends and I can have a private chat together but some of the big group chats get a bit nasty sometimes. I think because people know it's within the group only, it can get a bit gossipy and mean."

ELLA, 12

The use of messaging apps like WhatsApp, Snapchat and Instagram is on the rise. In fact, the latest research hints at a move away from Facebook to what are being called Social Chat apps. The pull of these apps is simple – they allow you to send pictures and comment to a select group of people you choose, which feels safer than broadcasting stuff across Facebook. Plus you can take part in private chatting and real-time chatting with a group of friends you select, without the whole world listening in.

However, these messaging apps bring their own problems. One of the main ones being cyberbullying – either by friends or anonymous people. As the app is not as public as Facebook, it can be easy to be sucked into a world of nastiness where people say things just because they can. That said, you can protect yourself from this by blocking users who annoy you and taunt you, and configuring your settings so you only accept messages from users on your 'My Friends' list instead of 'everyone'.

Also bear in mind the same rules apply to messaging apps as apply to all social networks (see What are you posting? on page 51 for more on this).

Be wary of location services and geotagging

"Do photos really have location information embedded in them when you post online?"

SI, 14

GPS and Wi-Fi on your smartphone, games console and laptop can let other people know exactly where you are. The same goes for location features on Twitter, Facebook and some apps. Most people love it because it allows you to tell others where you are, to get information on shops and brands nearby and possibly even discounts. Like everything, however, it has a potential downside. If, for instance, you post a lot of 'selfies' (self-portraits taken with your phone) and pictures of you out and about online, you're giving away a fair bit about you.

Due to geotagging – the process of adding geographical identification to various media such as photographs, video websites, text/picture messages – your GPS information is marked on all videos and photos you post. This means that someone could locate you if they wanted to.

Thankfully it's easy to change. All you have to do is turn the geotagging or location feature off on your phone. However, it's also important to tell your friends, especially if they tag you in pictures and post across a lot of sites. Bear in mind that you don't have to switch location off completely, if you want to use Google Maps for example – but you can select which applications can access GPS data and then reset. This way you're more in control of the information you're giving away, but still able to use location services.

20 ways to protect yourself online

1. *Never reveal information that can help someone find you in the real world (this includes geotagging on photos).*

2. *Always remember, no matter how nice someone seems online, they may not be who they seem so don't share too much.*

3. *Never write about personal, heartfelt issues and feelings online unless you want them broadcast to your entire school.*

4. *Don't assume your posts aren't being read or seen just because you have no comments. Everything you say and do online is seen by someone.*

5 *Avoid giving out very personal information such as your address, phone number and details on sign-up that could allow people to trace you.*

6 *Regulate what you say and do online in your head. This is the best form of privacy control.*

7 *Bear in mind that whatever you share can be shared again. This includes private pictures, gossip, news and also videos.*

8 *Protect your phone with a password. New phones are really computers and can store as much or even more personal information than your laptop or desktop.*

9 *Use different passwords for different sites, and email and messaging services. This way if one password gets into the wrong hands, the person won't be able to use it to access all your sites.*

10 *In chat rooms and multi-player gaming, always use a nickname that's different from your screen name. That way, if you ever find yourself in a conversation that makes you uncomfortable, you can leave without having to worry that someone knows your name and can track you down.*

11 *Be careful what you share with other networks. Linking everything to Facebook means you need to ensure that you have the same privacy settings across all your networks.*

12 *Don't post everything you think of to Facebook/ Twitter – saying you've copied someone's homework or are about to dump someone before you do is just asking for trouble.*

13 *Have regular 'friend' purges. Go through your friend lists and block anyone you don't know. It's likely you've completely forgotten who you're connected to and why.*

14 *If you're addicted to checking in wherever you go, think about what you're doing and when. Especially if you're on holiday abroad and your parents' house is empty! Or if you're skipping school and you don't want anyone to know.*

15 *If you want to stop people tagging you in embarrassing pictures on Facebook, you can do this by going to Account/Settings/Timeline and tagging and select all the options that give you control over what others post.*

16 *Always log out of social media sites if you're in a public place or at a friend's house. Just closing down the browser on a tablet, phone or laptop isn't enough because the next person who opens up the browser will be logged in as you.*

17 *Be wary of the local networks you join – for instance, school ones or ones based on a common interest – as it means every other member of that network will have access to your profile information (though you can change this in privacy settings).*

18 *Act the way you want others to act. It's no good complaining that someone posted a horrible picture of you and tagged everyone in, if you regularly do the same.*

19 *Be careful with online gaming chat. You should only be chatting about the game not personal details – be aware that you have no idea who you are talking to, or what their intentions are.*

20 *Respect other people's privacy. X may not want everyone to know she fancies Y. Or your best friend may not want everyone to know he can't talk to girls. If you want your privacy respected, don't be mean online.*

CHAPTER FIVE

The dark side

"Someone posts horrible things about me all the time. They say 'I'm nothing' and that 'I'm ugly' and that 'Everyone hates me'. The worst thing is I don't know who's doing it and it keeps happening day and night."

DAISY, 14

With all that's great and fantastic about technology, social media and the Internet, there is a dark side. While many people blame the technology itself and social media sites in the main, in reality it's people who are behind the negatives associated with the Internet. These are people who hide behind fake personas and who use anonymity to post horrible comments and bully. People who put up fake profiles to trick and groom others, and people who make others' online lives miserable just because they can.

While we're painting a pretty horrible view of the negatives, its important to understand and know what's out there, not only to avoid it, but also to be able to deal with it if it ever happens to you. For this reason, this chapter is about the dark side of tech: the people to avoid, the people to block and the smart tips that will help you to stay off their radar.

It's also about cyberbullying, Internet trolls (the really nasty people online) and people with very bad intentions. It is not designed to make you stay offline but simply to help you manage your presence more safely when you are online so that things don't go wrong.

QuiZ What scares you online?

1 *When setting up a social media profile, what do you do?*

- **a** Try and get as many friends as possible by accepting requests from friends, friends of friends and people you barely know
- **b** Lie about yourself to make yourself sound more exciting
- **c** Set up strict privacy settings

2 *You see a post where someone is being really nasty and mean about a subject you care about. What do you do?*

- **a** Jump in and get angry back
- **b** Ignore it as you don't want to get involved
- **c** Block that person

3 *All your friends start posting about this great place they went to. They didn't invite you but have tagged you into all the pictures. What do you do?*

- **a** Feel rejected and get angry with them
- **b** Feel they are doing it on purpose to make a point
- **c** Feel you are being bullied by them

4 *Someone you don't know starts chatting to you online. It starts off fun but then gets weird. What do you do?*

- **a** Feel uncomfortable but carry on talking to them
- **b** Ignore them and hope they go away
- **c** Get scared and switch off

5 *You make a comment on someone else's timeline and suddenly everyone is being mean to you. What do you do?*

- **a** Feel upset but these things happen
- **b** Feel upset and decide you're never going on the site in question again
- **c** See it as a sign that you're not ready for social media

6 *Someone anonymously sends a nasty video to you. Do you?*

- **a** Assume your account's been hacked
- **b** Assume your friends are winding you up
- **c** Assume someone's out to get you

7 *When it comes to age restrictions on sites and games, what do you do?*

- **a** Totally ignore them. If your friends are on them, so are you
- **b** Feel bad about ignoring them but do what your friends do
- **c** Feel scared about ignoring them but you often do to try them out

8 *When you're online do you ever feel scared about who's looking at your stuff?*

- **a** No never
- **b** Yes, you're afraid your parents are looking
- **c** Yes all the time

Mostly As You love being online so much that you don't give much thought to the negatives. You're willing just to jump in and say what you think to whoever you are speaking to. While this can be fun and exciting, you need to be more careful about who you are connected to, and also who you are talking to. If you're too concerned with the amount of friends or the amount of 'likes' you have, the end result will be that you'll attract the very people you should be avoiding online. Why? Well because not everyone is like you and not everyone has good intentions. Be careful.

Mostly Bs You're an equal mix of someone who both loves and is scared by what happens online. This isn't a bad place to be as it means you're aware that there are negatives and positives. However, what you need to realize is that you are not helpless in the face of the negatives. If something scares you or makes you upset, there are things you can do. Aside from blocking people and pulling people up on their online behaviour, there are a number of ways to deal with nastiness online. Don't just ignore it and hope it will go away.

Mostly Cs You are a worrier! Social media and technology are not things to be scared about. As we've said there is a dark side to the Internet but there are also lots of positives. Despite the news stories there isn't a strange person around every corner. In many ways if you do it correctly it's not only fun but also exciting. The trick is to start slowly, only connect to people you truly know and set privacy settings on all your accounts. This way you don't have to be afraid of encountering scary things or nasty people.

Trolls and trolling

Being online can do strange things to people. One of the main things it does is make people think that they can say and do anything they want without any repercussions. Much of this is down to the disconnect that happens when we aren't face-to-face with someone. The result is that some people's nastier instincts creep out and splatter all over the place. The name for this kind of person is a troll and they are the people who just want to wind up others, draw a reaction, bully with words and basically make people's lives a misery – often for no reason at all.

TROLL FACT *In its most extreme form, trolling is a criminal offence. One man was jailed after posting offensive messages and videos on tribute pages about young people who had died.*

It's likely that you've even come across a troll. They tend to be people who like to turn harmless discussions into nasty arguments and people who fill other people's timelines, message boards, tribute pages and newspaper comment sections with vicious, spiteful comments, insulting jokes and bad-taste insults and threats.

So why do trolls do it?

1 *Anonymity is a massive factor. Trolls can be as aggressive, rude and unpleasant as they like when they are anonymous because there are no immediate*

consequences as there would be in real life. When people know they are anonymous, they are more likely to do things they otherwise wouldn't. Whether that's throwing out a negative comment, being overly nasty or picking on people they don't even know. Evidence definitely points to this as trolling completely fell off the charts when one UK newspaper (The Times) *put up a paywall. This meant you had to register and pay to get on the site, which took away all anonymity from people using it.*

TROLL FACT *Trolls are usually (but not always) young adult males who do it for amusement, boredom and/or revenge.*

2 *Studies show that when you can't see the person on the other end of the comments, your inhibitions become lowered and this makes people more aggressive and rude than they usually would be.*

3 *Trolls also know there are no immediate repercussions for leaving a nasty, vile or threatening comment. Most trolls just drop something into the mix and run away, or stay and keep trying to get a reaction from the person they are trolling.*

4 *Some trolls see being in cyberspace as a game where they can act any way they want to anyone they want.*

5 *Some trolls do it for pure personal amusement – getting a kick from the fact that they are hurting, worrying or upsetting someone.*

6 *Other trolls do it for revenge and personal gain – though this tends to fall into the realm of cyberbullying.*

7 *Breaking taboos is another reason why some people troll. Shocking others by being deliberately insensitive about sensitive topics, like someone's death, suicide or sexuality, is a favourite 'hobby' of some trolls.*

8 *Boredom. Some trolls just do it because they're bored and like to wind others up.*

TROLLING FACT *More than one in ten people in the UK know someone who has suffered anonymous online abuse or so-called 'trolling', according to a new survey by YouGov.*

If you are ever tempted to troll, it's worth bearing in mind The Communications Act 2003. This governs the Internet, email, mobile phone calls and text messaging. Under section 127 of the act it is an offence to send messages that are 'grossly offensive or of an indecent, obscene or menacing character'. The offence occurs whether those targeted actually receive the message or not.

As for how to deal with a troll, the best way is to:

* *Immediately tell friends and family what's going on – trolls can be frightening and intimidating, and even when you have switched off, their words can linger.*

* *Report any anonymous abuse or intimidation to the social network, site owner, or if it's really serious, the police. Trolls think they are untouchable but they're not as their IP address (where the message came from) can be tracked.*

* *Do not reply or retaliate to a troll as it can make things worse.*
* *Consider blocking all users that send abusive or nasty messages.*
* *Keep a record of any aggressive or intimidating messages, posts, pictures or videos that you receive or see.*

Cyberbullying

"It went on for nearly six months and by the end, every time my phone went off I would flinch. I became so afraid that I wouldn't use my phone or computer. Then my teacher saw a message pop up when we were in ICT and she went mad at the girl who sent it. She then spoke to my mum and together they totally shut the bullies down. I only wish I had spoken up sooner."

JADA, 14

We all know what bullying is and how it looks in real life, but online it can be invasive and so constant that you can feel you can't escape it anywhere. Below are some of the ways people are cyberbullied (usually a number of these techniques are used):

* *Name-calling*
* *Rumour-spreading*
* *Being mean*
* *Being exclusive online*

* *Tagging horrible pictures of you*
* *Making mean jokes at your expense*
* *Anonymous, threatening or nasty messages being sent at all hours on social media sites, via text and direct messaging*
* *Sending abusive texts, video or photo messages*
* *Sharing videos of physical attacks*
* *Sexting*
* *Posting photos, personal information or fake comments*
* *Pretending to be someone online without that person's permission*

Cyberbullying is defined as 'when someone uses technology to deliberately hurt, humiliate, harass, intimidate or threaten someone else'. This action is done on purpose and repeated. Bullying literally crushes

people and in some cases makes them ill or suicidal. It breaks people's confidence and esteem, and affects everything from how they sleep and eat to how they perform in school. In many cases it makes people feel as if their life isn't worth living any more.

Like real-life bullying, cyberbullying is made worse either by the people who stand by and watch it happen or by those who participate in what's going on. If you know someone who is being bullied online, tell an adult what is going on. If you're tempted to add your own negative comments when people are being mean online, or share what's happening to other friends, don't. Instead, imagine how alienating and upsetting it would feel if everyone ganged up on you online.

CYBERBULLYING FACT
88% of teens say they have witnessed people being mean and cruel to others on social networking sites. 15% say they have been the target.

Normal bullying aside, there are a number of other ways people can be bullied online. 'Slut shaming' is when others shame or attack a girl for her relationship behaviour, for acknowledging or acting on sexual feelings. This is done by setting up specific pages on social networks where users can name people they consider worthy of the list.

Slut shaming is not only sexist (as it's aimed primarily at girls) but it's hugely damaging to the girls and women targeted, and also to women in general. If you're tempted to do this to someone for revenge, because you feel they deserve it or because you want to, think again.

Two Swedish teenagers were recently convicted of aggravated defamation for their role in a 'slut-shaming' that resulted in teen rioting. The girls, aged 15 and 16, were sentenced for having set up an account on Instagram that encouraged users to publish pictures of those they deemed 'sluts', along with descriptions of their alleged activities. It may well have its own name but this is cyberbullying at its worst.

What to do if you're being cyberbullied:

1. *The first thing to do is keep everything you are sent and messaged. This is evidence and also a way to track down your bullies.*
2. *Block the people bullying you. For instance, on Facebook you can block someone to prevent them from starting conversations with you or seeing things you post on your timeline. However, bear in mind that people you block can still see and comment on stuff you share with groups and shared friends.*
3. *If you're being bullied through various sites, or via text and/or email, change your phone number and email account, then shut down your activity on all sites until it is sorted out.*
4. *If you're being bullied through your phone, remember all UK mobile companies are used to dealing with nuisance calls and will have people you can contact to help you deal with this. Help yourself by not answering any calls that are from a withheld number and turn off your voicemail (your service provider can tell you how to do this). While mobile phone operators can't bar a particular number from contacting another phone, they can take action on*

the bully's account if they have been harassing and threatening you, such as blocking it.

5 *Tell someone what is happening. Cyberbullying is often worse than real-world bullying, simply because you can't get away from it no matter where you turn. It can also happen 24/7 and make you feel as if you are being tormented at every moment. Telling someone what is happening not only stops you feeling helpless but also puts you on the road to stopping the bullies for good.*

Illegal activity and content

Despite what people think, the Internet is not some lawless world where anything goes. Although it's global and the laws are more complicated (because what's illegal here may not be illegal in the US, for example) there are many activities that have criminal consequences. Illegal activity includes theft, online harassment and grooming (see page 87).

Illegal content includes images of child sex abuse and obscene images. It's important to know this as you may come across it and be very shocked and upset by it. Many people think it's funny to send vile (this could be graphically violent or sexual) images or videos as a joke or post them on their timeline.

If this happens, always tell someone what you have seen so they can reassure you. Images have a lot of power and they can stick in your mind long after you have seen or watched something and continue to upset you (or make you afraid of something). If you are worried that you're in danger or someone else is, tell a parent and the police.

Sharing information

One of the main worries for parents is that it's now possible for you to access the online world in a number of ways, from smartphones to gaming consoles and laptops. This gives everyone a huge number of ways to share everything from pictures and videos to personal information – often without thinking. Consider this – how often have you posted something online and then immediately regretted it? Probably a fair few times and it is this immediacy and this spontaneous behaviour that can get us into trouble.

The problem with being online is that we often forget to take the same precautions that we would in real life. So we start talking to someone we don't know, tell them intimate private things that we rarely tell others and maybe even share pictures and videos of ourselves via smartphones and webcams. You might not think you'd ever be this silly, but just take a look at your list of Facebook friends and consider how many you really know. It's likely there are at least ten people you don't know – that's ten people and their friends seeing your pictures, private information and commenting and chatting to you.

While online friendships (being friends with people you have only ever met online) can be rewarding and fun, becoming friends and trusting people you don't know in real life is a scary business. One TV show highlights this fact by trying to connect two online friends every episode. In 99% of cases, one of the people (sometimes both) has lied about everything from their profile picture and their age and name, to relationship status and even their sex.

Grooming

The ease with which the Internet allows you to be both fake and lie is worth bearing in mind before you start befriending people (whether on a multi-player game or a social media site). Exposing too much information to others can leave you at risk of grooming. This is a very manipulative process where an adult with sexual

FACT *In 2012 there were 1,000 reports a month to the Child Exploitation and Online Protection Centre related to online grooming and online sexual abuse.*

interest in children uses online sites and gaming forums to befriend you, gain your trust (usually by telling you that they understand you, that you're special and that they get you while no one else does) and make you feel as if you can't say no to them. They may pretend to be the same age as you, or that they like the same music and TV as you. Then as they gain your trust, they may ask you to do things that make you feel uncomfortable. Things like sharing pictures or saying things you don't want to and, more dangerously, arranging to meet them in real life.

FACT *Research by EU Kids Online shows that a third of kids in the UK have had contact online with people they have never met before.*

The key to avoiding all of this is to ensure that you never wholly trust anyone online that you don't know well in real life. Even if you feel a real connection to them and have shared pictures (pictures can be fake remember) and all kinds of information that make you think they are who they say they are, it could still be fake. Alongside this, if someone's online behaviour makes you feel uncomfortable then block them and tell an adult what's happening. Never, ever arrange to meet an online friend without telling your parents first – you may think you'll be able to protect yourself if it goes wrong, but why even take that risk? Put your safety first at all times.

The problem with online pornography

We all know pornography is everywhere on the Internet, but it's also posted daily all over social networking sites. While you are very unlikely to see it on Facebook, where there are stricter controls, that doesn't mean you won't come across a pornographic posting, a disturbing video or a Facebook group. On other social networking sites, pornography is rife and while it's tempting to share it for a 'laugh', be wary of what you're doing.

According to a study from Canada, 90% of male students aged 14–17 years and 70% of females of the same age reported accessing sexually explicit media content at least once on the Internet. While curiosity is normal, it's also very important to be aware that looking constantly at pornographic images ultimately affects how you feel about your body, future relationships and sex. Many of these images are also taken and posted without consent, which is another important factor to consider if you're reposting them.

Remember, if you see an offensive picture or video that has been posted on a social networking site, you can report it to the site. Facebook, for instance, has an Abuse & Spam page where you can report inappropriate photos, comments or users that are in violation of Facebook's guidelines and terms of use.

10 ways to stay safe online

1 **Pay attention to age ratings.**
Whether you like them or not, they are there for a purpose. Apps, Facebook and more importantly games have age-restricted ratings.

2 **Don't try to outsmart parental controls.**
No filter is ever perfect and you probably know a million ways to get round controls, but consider why you're doing it. There is some stuff on the Internet that is truly so disturbing that you will never want to see it.

3 **Stay off adult sites.**
Certain sites like porn sites attract people sharing very adult content. These sites say you have to be 18 to enter and while it's easy to lie, think about what you will be exposing yourself to.

4 **If someone is being horrible, nasty or provocative shut them down.**
Block them on Facebook, unfollow them on Twitter, or block them from your contact book.

5 **Listen to your gut.**
If someone is saying something online that feels wrong or uncomfortable then trust your judgment and back away. If you feel scared or threatened by someone's online behaviour, immediately tell an adult who can help.

6 Think about your privacy.
See Chapter 4 for more on this. Don't give out information in any form that people you don't know (or even do know) can use to get to you or use against you.

7 Don't think if you ignore it, it will go away.
Cyberbullies work on harassment in that they will keep going on and on at you, trying to break your spirit until you do something.

8 Don't worry about getting into trouble with parents.
Sometimes you may not want to say that something horrible is happening because you weren't meant to be on Facebook or somewhere else in the first place. All parents will want to know what's going on, regardless of whether or not you have broken a rule.

9 Don't befriend people you don't know.
This is easier said than done as sometimes you know someone through someone and feel as if they should be a 'friend.'

10 If you feel threatened, harassed or scared and frightened in any way by someone's behaviour online, contact the police.

Help section

These organizations' websites have more help and advice for staying safe online. Many of the websites have contact details if you need to talk to someone or have questions.

AskAboutGames
http://www.askaboutgames.com
Advice and tips about video game age ratings, how to play games responsibly, and potential problems.

Bullying UK
http://www.bullying.co.uk
For help with cyberbullying and bullying.

Centre For Internet Addiction
http://www.netaddiction.com
Counselling for those addicted to the Internet and their families.

Child Exploitation and Online Protection Centre
http://ceop.police.uk
National crime agency aiming to stop online child sex offenders. Information section for parents, carers and guardians.

Childine
http://www.childline.org.uk/explore/bullying/pages/cyberbullying.aspx
Childline's advice pages on coping with cyberbullying.

ChatDanger
http://www.chatdanger.com
How to stay safe while chatting online.

Common Sense Media
http://www.commonsensemedia.org
Information and safety help for anyone who is online.

Facebook
https://www.facebook.com/safety
How to stay safe on Facebook.

Internet Safety For Parents
http://internet-safety.yoursphere.com
Information for parents on tech.

Quibly
http://quib.ly/welcome
Parenting tech site answering every question you could possibly have about your kids online.

Safe Kids
http://www.safekids.com
How to stay safe online.

Safer Internet
http://www.saferinternet.org.uk
Tips, advice and resources to help you stay safe online.

Think U Know
http://www.thinkuknow.co.uk
Tips and advice about staying safe online.

* The website addresses (URLs) included in this book were valid at the time of going to press. However, because of the nature of the Internet, it is possible that some addresses may have changed, or sites may have changed or closed down since publication. While the author and publishers regret any inconvenience this may cause the readers, no responsibility for any such changes can be accepted by either the author or the publisher.

Glossary

Age rating – the age at which a social network, game or app is applicable.

Apps – self-contained software programmes used on a smartphone, tablet or computer. They can be a game, a map, music software, or absolutely anything.

Chat acronym – an acronym used to communicate, usually through instant messaging and texting. Some popular acronyms include LOL (laugh out loud) and MorF (male or female).

Cyberbullying – bullying through Internet applications and technologies such as instant messaging (IM), social networking sites, texts and smartphones.

IM – instant messaging or online chat in real time.

Geotagging – the process of adding geographical identification to media you are posting, such as photos and video.

Grooming – the process that predators use to manipulate minors into sexual relationships or into producing sexual images of themselves. It often includes the giving of compliments or gifts.

Hacker – someone who accesses computer information either legally or illegally.

Hashtags – words preceded by a # sign. On Twitter these can be used to tie various tweets together and relate them to a topic – be it a conference, TV show, sporting event, or any happening or trend of your choosing. Twitter automatically links all hashtags so that users can search for other tweets using the same tag.

History – a list of sites that the people using a particular computer/smartphone have visited.

Profile – social media sites often call for users to create a profile where they share certain information, such as their real names, hobbies and interests. Facebook and MySpace users create a profile when they join the sites.

Sexting – the use of mobile phones to send sexual messages, pictures and videos.

Smartphones – phones with operating systems that allow users to run applications similar to those used on computers.

Social network – an online community where people set up profiles and befriend, or friend, each other.

Troll – an anonymous person who causes trouble on social networks or in general on the Internet. Trolls tend to pick on well-known people, or say sexist, homophobic or racist things just to stir up trouble.

Index